# Love Notes
## to a
# DEAR
## DAUGHTER

Jalia Kangave

*For Nnanda and Nsanji.*
*And Sophia and Zara.*
*And Amira, Kailah and Tara.*
*And Lianne and Laura.*
*For Pascale, Alliance and Martha.*
*And Lumiere, Celeste and Niki*

---

*And all the wonderful girls and young women who we*
*have the blessing to call our daughters.*

# CONTENTS

# PREFACE

Dear daughter,

In a lovely school in Brighton called Downs Infant School, reception class children are taught a song:

*With my eyes and ears and hands and feet,*
*I am marvellously made*
*With a brain to think and a heart that beeps,*
*in every single way*
*I'm a miracle,*
*I'm a miracle, an amazing creation you see*
*I'm remarkable and incredible*
*I'm a miracle*
*That's me!*

There is a playfulness and simpleness in the choice of the words of this song that speaks directly to the heart and the mind of a four-year old. And yet, there is also a profoundness in the message that is often lost on us, particularly as we grow older. That is, that each and every one of us is a miracle. That each and every one of us is precious and valuable and worthy. I have found myself singing this song out loudly or nibbling on it delicately every time I am threatened with feelings of unworthiness. And almost every time I sing it, it tickles my heart and awakens my spirit. It reminds me of how incredibly precious I am. How incredibly precious we all are.

Dear daughter, I hope that you don't just learn the words of this song, but that you also live it. Sing it. Walk it. Breathe it. Believe it. Because, whatever is going on in your life right now, whatever doubts or fears or insecurities you may have, whatever battles you are fighting or may have lost, it is important that you remember that you are a miracle. You are incredible. And remarkable. And most beautifully made.

The celebrated author and civil rights activist, Maya Angelou, often said, "When you learn, teach." Inside this book, I share with you some of the lessons that I have learnt over the past 42 years. In here, you will find my 5-year-old self who believed in magic before she was saddled with the burdens of adulthood. You will encounter the teenage me who suffered from numerous insecurities and the 20-year-old me who, in spite of her insecurities, still believed that she could change the world. You will also engage with my thirty-something year old self who constantly beat herself up for the many mistakes that she had made in the past and the ones she continued to make in her thirties. Lastly, you will be in conversation with the 42-year-old me, who still makes mistakes, falls into traps of anxiety, still double-guesses herself and yet is more gentle with herself, more forgiving of herself and more patient with herself – and in turn, challenged to be more forgiving, more gentle and more patient with others.

# One
## YOU ARE ENOUGH

ONE DAY, WHEN I was about twelve or thirteen years old, I was having a heated argument with an older male cousin. I must have been winning the argument. Because he felt the need to tell me that I was not beautiful and that I would need to work really hard to succeed in life. Coming from a male figure that I looked up to, those words pierced my heart and punctured my confidence. I began to see myself as only one thing: not beautiful. And I imagined that everyone who saw me, saw what my cousin had seen. I spent the rest of my teenage years and the bulk of the years that would follow trying to make up for my lack of beauty. I got into relationships that I shouldn't have, exposed myself to abuse that I did not deserve and desperately and frequently tried to compensate for the beauty that I had been informed I lacked. It was not until my late thirties that I came to the realisation that I was enough. That only I could define my beauty. Only I could determine my worth. That what really mattered was not what others thought of me but what I thought of myself.

Dear daughter, you may be feeling that you are not enough: not beautiful enough, not thin enough, perhaps too fat or too thin, or too dark, maybe not even intelligent enough. I know that feeling. And I know the suffering that accompanies it. For far too long, I lived a life of "not enoughness". Of looking for – and finding – fault with myself. Of not loving myself. Of not thinking that I was loveable. After decades, this is what I know for sure: that when we look for fault in ourselves, we shall surely find it. That when we allow others to reduce us to simplistic definitions of beauty, we let them violate our most sacred of spaces – our soul. I have found that there are several ways in which we can belittle ourselves and assist others in belittling us. What we need to do instead is to get into the habit of loving ourselves. No one can do that part of the work for us. Because even when we find someone who loves us, their love is not able to access and heal our hidden and most intimate wounds.

I hope, dear daughter, that you will start the work of loving yourself much earlier than I did. Because it is such a liberating feeling when you fall in love with you. I promise you. Try it. Because you are worth it. And because you are enough.

*Two*

# TEACH PEOPLE
# HOW TO TREAT YOU

MY FIVE-YEAR OLD DAUGHTER once came home with an invitation to a birthday party of a boy in her class. When we opened the invitation, she said, "Maama, I don't want to go to that party." (My daughters love parties!) I asked her why. She said, "Because X (the boy) is mean to me." I asked, "How?" She said, "He called me stupid and pushed me." I held onto the invitation for a couple of days – because little people have fights and call each other names and then are best friends the next minute. After two days, I asked her if she was sure that she didn't want to go to X's party. Without hesitation, she said, "Yes, I am sure." I sent our regrets to X's mother.

There will be times when you will be tempted to let things go because you are afraid that when you act on your instinct, you will become less likeable. Other times, you may just feel the need to be polite even to people who have abused you – in whatever form. And sometimes, you may even be led to believe that you deserve to be treated poorly.

People will generally treat you the way you let them treat you. When someone calls you stupid and pushes you and you still turn up for their birthday party, who knows what they will do next? It starts by exposing yourself to the seemingly small transgressions – laughing nervously when someone tells a distasteful joke about you in front of their friends, smiling when they sneakily pinch your buttocks (even when it makes you feel uncomfortable) and saying, "it's okay" when it really is not okay. Soon, you will be making excuses for the partner who cheats on you, you will find a reason to explain why they beat you and before you know it, you will not be able to recognise yourself because you will be living in the shadow of someone else.

Draw the line early enough. Say, "I will not go to X's party because X called me stupid and pushed me." Teach people how to treat you. Let them know that you deserve to be treated with dignity.

## Three

# DO NOT SHRINK YOURSELF
# TO ACCOMMODATE
# FRAGILE EGOS

WHEN I WAS GETTING ready to start my Masters degree, an older male cousin warned me: "You are going to have a hard time finding a husband. You are already a lawyer. Now you are going to do a Masters degree?!" I smiled. I went ahead and got my Masters. And then I did my PhD. I was not trying to prove anything to my cousin. I was simply fulfilling my heart's desires.

Do not give up your dreams for fear of intimidating a man or anyone for that matter. Similarly, do not shrink yourself in order to fit into fragile egos. If your ambitions are too big for some people, then those are not the people for you. There are many things that will shatter fragile egos – it could be your education, your career success or even simply, your joyfulness. Whatever you do, those who suffer from fragility will be threatened. So do the things that bring you fulfilment.

## *Four*

# FORGIVE YOURSELF FOR PAST MISTAKES

YOU ARE GOING TO make several mistakes in your life. Things that may bring you shame or heartache. Things that make you cringe when you give them too much attention. Try not to beat yourself up over these mistakes. Be gentle with yourself. Forgive yourself as many times as you need to. If need be, confide in and seek counsel in a trusted friend. And then, work on doing better. As Maya Angelou often said, "When you know better, you do better."

## *Five*
# DON'T STOP READING

DEAR DAUGHTER, DON'T STOP reading. You will find that books are wonderful companions. They will not just enrich you with new knowledge. They will also heal you and nourish your soul. They will make you cry and they will make you laugh. They will open your mind and they will embolden your footsteps. They will take you on journeys around the world and they will bring you back to yourself. They will help you develop more compassion for others and they will remind you of the many things that you ought to be grateful for. Most of all, they will remind you of how alike we all are.

## *Six*
# YOUR HAPPINESS IS YOUR RESPONSIBILITY

I HAVE ALREADY SAID that it is your duty to love yourself. You will also eventually realise that it is your responsibility to make yourself happy. Other people can enrich your experiences. However, they cannot complete you. They may cheer you up. But they cannot sustain you. I have found that when we rely on others to make us happy, we set ourselves up for huge disappointment and many times, heavy heartache. Similarly, to require or expect another person to be responsible for our happiness is to deposit a heavy and unfair burden on them. It is not another person's job to make you happy.

Identify the things that tickle your heart. The things that nourish your soul. The things that lift your spirit and make you laugh and smile. They need not be expensive– indeed many times they are free: a walk in the park, a run through the woods, a good book, volunteering at your local school, listening to soulful music, dancing to the beats of drums. It is always in the little things that big magic is experienced.

## Seven
# DON'T STOP SINGING

I HOPE YOU DON'T stop singing. As a young girl, I loved singing. I would sing at the top of my lungs, without a care of what I sounded like and oblivious of who was listening. When I run out of songs to sing, I would compose my own songs and teach them to my younger siblings (who did not have much of a choice over whether or not they wanted to join my band). But somewhere along the way, I stopped singing. I became more conscious about the sound of my voice. And I became less playful. Am not sure exactly when this happened but it certainly had to do with growing up. I was led to believe that people would only take me seriously if I put on a tough exterior. I forgot the joy of voicing out song. I forgot the creativity that was sparked by play. And I forgot the therapy of hearty laughter. I started to hide my smile and quieten my voice. I lost the child in me who was so essential in dealing with the adult world.

I hope you don't stop singing baby girl. I hope you continue being playful, remember to laugh out loud and to dance to the beats of drums. Even when you grow up. Indeed, particularly when you grow up. Because there are going to be many opportunities in your life to showcase your seriousness – some even unwelcome and heart breaking. So, play and sing and dance and laugh every so often. Grow up but stay youthful and playful.

## *Eight*
## SEX IS NOT LOVE

DEAR DAUGHTER, DO NOT confuse sex with love. Do not have sex out of fear that someone will leave you. Do not rush into sex because "everybody is doing it". There are no rewards for getting there before others or with others. Do not engage in sex believing that it will make you more desirable; more loveable. You already are worthy and your body is sacred. Do not use it to compensate for the things that you feel you are lacking. Do not use it out of fear that you are not enough. And do not use it to fill a void or as payback.

## *Nine*

# YOU DO NOT NEED
# TO BE STRONG

FOR A LONG TIME, it was impressed upon me that as a woman, I was expected to exhibit strength. I heard women who were experiencing hardships in their relationships being told: "*guma*" (be strong). Every now and then, I hear someone (a man or a woman) lament: "What happened to the women of this generation? They are not as strong as our mothers used to be." Recently, I was speaking with a friend about another friend who had lost her mother. When I asked about how our friend was holding up, my friend said: "Oh, X is very strong. She has barely even cried." In many ways, the strength of a woman is equated with her goodness. A strong woman is a woman to be admired. A strong woman is a good woman.

A strong woman, it appears, is one who is able to withstand hardship without developing creases. A woman who smiles through her pain and single-handedly resolves her problems. A strong woman braves the challenges that she experiences in her relationship: work that breaks her back, a partner who ignores her needs, fears that occupy her mind and abuse that belittles and undermines her value. When she gets married, she stays married. Divorce is not in her vocabulary. She experiences little or no struggle in raising her children. She doesn't need to yell at them because she has mastered a calmness and an inner peace that allow her to be assertive without being aggressive. When her little children appear in public, they present in well-pressed clothes and neatly manicured nails. At home, she makes freshly cooked meals from scratch and her house is squeaky clean. A strong woman is one whose womanhood does not get in the way of her performance at work. She doesn't bring up the illness of her child to explain her inability to meet a deadline. She does not utilise her full maternity leave because this may jeopardise her promotion. And she forces a smile throughout the staff Christmas party because, while she would really rather be at home tucking her children into bed, she needs to demonstrate that family does not get in the way of work. If the men can do it, she can do it.

Before I knew what it really took to be a strong/good woman, I aspired to be one. I would be the wife who did not complain, the mother who did not yell and the employee whose performance was not affected by her personal obligations. But after five years of marriage, two children and several years of work, I realised that I am the mother who sometimes yells even after promising myself that I will not do it again. I was also the academic who was not capable to churning out publishable papers every six months when I also needed to be available to help my daughters with their school projects and enjoy weekends with them at the park without worrying about deadlines. And I was the wife who was incapable of remaining cheerful after having carried the bulk of housework and childcare.

I came to the conclusion that I was not a strong woman. In fact, I decided that I did not desire to be one. This version of womanhood denied my womanhood. It required that I choke my tears, deny my fears and be ashamed of my humanly and womanly struggles. In other words, it required me to harden. I realised that the women that I admire the most are the women who make their scars and struggles visible to me. The women who are courageous enough to say, "Today has been a hard day. I am struggling." The women who constantly ask for help with school drop-offs and pick-ups. The women who feel guilty about yelling at their children "yet again". The women who admit that they feel lost after the death of a spouse. The women who let their tears flow out when they feel pain. In other words, all the women who are not afraid to express their raw humanity. The women who have given me permission not to be superwoman.

Dear daughter, do not be led to believe that as a woman, or indeed as a human being, your value is measured based on your hardness. That you need to suffer in silence in order to prove that you are an admirable version of a woman. That breaking your back and enduring hardship are some form of martyrdom. That your worth is measured by how much you can endure and how long you can endure it for. That a woman who is worthy is the one who can keep a squeaky clean house, show up with her thinking cap perfectly fit on for work, take great care of her children and satisfy her man's needs, all while smiling and without complaining. I will tell you now, dear daughter, that there is no need for you to be a superwoman. There are no superwoman awards. And there is no disgrace in being less than perfect. So, stop when you need to rest. Say no when you don't feel like doing something. Cry when you feel pain. Sit down and do nothing. The world will not come to an end.

## Ten

# REMEMBER TO ASK
# FOR HELP

YESTERDAY I WAS REMINDED of why we do not have to figure life out on our own. I had been looking at our garden for months and feeling overwhelmed every time I thought about the work that would need to go into making it look decent. Feeling defeated, a couple of weeks ago, I asked our neighbour, Sheila, whether she knew of a gardener who could come and help us tidy it up. Sheila said: "Oh darling, you don't need to bring in a gardener. That would cost you too much! Why don't we get a day for me to come over so that we can work on it together and then you can figure out whether you still need a gardener." Yesterday, Sheila turned up at 10am with her big smile, some bin bags and hands full of gardening tools. From 10am to 1.30pm, we worked and we laughed. We sweated and we talked. We joked and we reminisced. We gulped down litres of water and bit into scrumptious sandwiches.

Our garden looks much better now.

But that is beside the point. My point is that it is okay to ask for help. It is okay not to have to figure life out on your own. The idea of self-sufficiency and the "I can do it on my own" attitude is killing us. We do not need to quarantine ourselves from the rest of the world. Because when we do, our problems seem much bigger than they actually are. Our challenges a lot more insurmountable. We were made for connection. For inter-dependence. Let the people around you know when you need help. Be okay with saying, "I am struggling. I need your help." Because when you do, people respond with "We are here. How may we serve you?"

*Eleven*

# DON'T FORGET WHERE
# YOU CAME FROM

I WASN'T ALWAYS PROUD of my identity and particularly, not my culture. I was the girl who took pride in not speaking Luganda fluently. The girl who smiled delightfully when my relatives would say, "Oh, that one doesn't know Luganda. You need to speak with her in English." One semester, when I was in graduate school in Canada, students in my hall of residence were planning for a cultural show. I realised then that unlike many of the other students – a good number of whom were international students like me – I did not know much about my culture. I was not able to perform any of our cultural dances. I was not in position to narrate any of our folktales. Neither did I have stories relating to the healing properties of our herbal medicines. And I was not, of course, able to speak fluent Luganda. Needless to say, I was terribly embarrassed. I felt like I did not belong.

In the years that followed, I noted the pride with which my Iranian sister, Shiva, talked about their poetry and shared their love for pistachio nuts. I observed the confidence and pride with which my Nigerian sisters, Ibironke and Mosope, carried around their Yoruba names. And I paid attention to how Chinese families brought grandparents to Vancouver to teach their grandchildren Mandarin. Meanwhile, here I was, more comfortable in English than I was in Luganda. Knowing more about hip-hop than I knew about *amagunju*. I felt a kind of poverty that I had never felt before in my life. I realised then that no amount of education or exposure could make me run away from myself, my people. That unless I was rooted in my history and my origin, I really did not belong anywhere.

Take the time, dear daughter, to find out more about your origin. Where do your ancestors come from? What language do your people speak? Do you know about your folklores? What about the stories of the great warriors and wise leaders of your people? What foods are most common and which spices are most treasured? What are the healing properties of the herbs that grow in your village? Sit at the feet of elders. Ask questions. Bury yourself in the books of history. Visit museums of anthropology. Watch documentaries. Travelling to the past will help you understand and appreciate the present.

*Twelve*

# SPEAK KINDLY TO YOURSELF

DEVELOP THE HABIT OF speaking kindly to yourself. Tell yourself what a lovely person you are. What a beautiful person you are. What a wonderful and incredible person you are. What a funny and intelligent person you are. What a good friend, a great daughter, a loving sister you are. Love and speak kindly to your body. Honour it for allowing you to travel through the years. For allowing you to see the world. For allowing you to feel. Do not bash yourself. Do not speak unkindly to or of your body. Do not belittle yourself. There will be people and experiences out there that will do that unpleasant job. Don't join them.

## *Thirteen*
# DEVELOP THE COURAGE
# TO SPEAK UP AGAINST
# WRONG

DEAR DAUGHTER, DEVELOP THE courage to speak up against injustice and the character to treat people with dignity and kindness. Courage, you will find, is not necessarily defined by big acts and loud noises. It starts with the seemingly small things. Like refusing to laugh at jokes that are intended to belittle someone. Or abstaining from engaging in gossip that is aimed at judging another. Or sharing your point of view, even when you are in the minority and without any guarantees that it will be taken on board. Or speaking, even when your heart is beating fast and your voice is shaking. As Maya Angelou often said, when we start to exercise our courage muscles in these seemingly small ways, we gain the courage to speak up about the bigger things.

## Fourteen
# YOUR VOICE MATTERS

DO YOU SUFFER FROM the imposter syndrome? Do you sometimes fear to put your hand up in class because you think that your questions are silly or your answers are wrong? Do you refrain from speaking up in meetings because you fear that your contributions will not sound intelligent enough? Well, I did (and indeed, sometimes, I still do). For a very long time, I did not think that my ideas mattered. I thought that my answers were wrong and that my questions were silly. And so, many times, I kept quiet in meetings and in class. And then I wanted to kick myself when someone else said what I had wanted – but feared – to say. Over time, I have learnt that my voice matters. That there are no silly questions. That my views could have a positive impact on someone else's life. And even though I still second-guess myself every now and then, I have learnt to put my message out there and let the universe decide what it means to them.

## *Fifteen*
## LOVE IS NOT PAIN

DEAR DAUGHTER, I HAVE an intelligent, beautiful and vivacious friend whose eye sockets were plucked out by her estranged husband. She is now blind. My other friend's sister was killed by a jealous husband. She was just in her early twenties. She left behind two daughters, who are now teenagers. And one of my cousins died in her late twenties after contracting AIDS from her unfaithful husband.

These might seem like extreme examples. They might also seem like incidents that are unlikely to happen to you or to people who are like you. Yet they are more common than we think. Every day, thousands of women around the world are killed, maimed or emotionally scarred by men who claim to love them. These women are educated and they are uneducated. They are black and white and brown. They are employed and they are unemployed. They are thin and fat. They are rich and they are poor. They are loud and they are soft-spoken.

Always remember, dear daughter, that there is no justification for anyone physically or mentally abusing you. A man who hurts you does not love you. A man who beats you does not love you. A man who calls you names and belittles you does not love you. It does not matter how many flowers he buys you or how expensive the gifts that he showers you with are. It does not matter how much he says he loves you. The expression of love is not in the things that he gives you or the words that he utters. It is in the way that he treats you.

Now, it is never easy to walk away from an abusive relationship. That is why you do not need to walk that journey alone. Seek the help of a trusted friend or an elder or a professional. Reach out for support. There will be a community and a life waiting for you on the other side.

*Sixteen*

# NOT ALL MEN CHEAT

YOU MAY HAVE HEARD statements like "all men cheat" or "all men are dogs". Those statements are simply not true. While it is true that there are men who cheat on their women, it is also true that there are men who respect their commitment and vows to women. Do not lower your standards by starting from a place of limitations. You attract what you believe. When you start from a place of scarcity or negativity, you settle for less because subconsciously, you internalise the message that you deserve less. Know that you are worthy, which includes being worthy of a respectful and loving relationship.

## *Seventeen*
# TAKE GOOD CARE OF YOUR BODY

TAKE GOOD CARE OF your body. Accustom it to movement through play, dance and exercise. Treat it to a good night's sleep to allow it to relax and rejuvenate. Replenish it with fruits and vegetables and fresh juices and water. Love it. In whatever shape or form it comes. It is your sacred space.

*Eighteen*
# GUARD YOUR MENTAL SPACE

L EARN TO GUARD YOUR mental space. It is, perhaps, your most sacred of spaces. Protect your mind and your heart from people and things that intend to peck at you; to bring you down; to distract you from your goals and to cause you harm. Maya Angelou once told Oprah Winfrey, when she (Oprah) was complaining about what had been said about her in the media, "Oprah, you are not in it. People will try to peck you to death like a duck. But remember, you're not in it."

When you start to feel disappointed or discouraged or disheartened by something that someone says about you, remind yourself that you are not in it. You might not be able to control what people say or think about you. But you get to determine how you react to it. You get to decide what you let in and who you let into your sacred space. You get to say, "I will not be a part of that conversation" or "I do not want to be around that person" – "It is, or they are, too toxic for me. I am not in it."

## Nineteen
# RUN YOUR OWN RACE

AS I TAKE MY morning walks through the beautiful greenery of Preston Park, I am reminded of the rich tapestry that is life. Some of us are walking and some of us are running. Some of us are fast while some of us are slow. Some of us are in front and some of us are behind. Some of us are running East and some of us are running West. Each of us is "running" our own race.

There have been times when I have been tempted to run and catch up with the others. When I have been distracted by the journeys of others. When I start to get into a panic for fear of being left behind. And then, my body reminds me that that is not my race.

In my apparent slowness, in my seeming inability to catch up with others, I have found the roadmap to my own journey. My unhurried walks have been the pen strokes through which ideas have been birthed and bathed. My slow strides have been the funnel through which I have reached into my inner and most evolving being. And my apparent lagging has cultivated the humility through which I view and perceive others.

We are living in an era in which technology has made it increasingly difficult for us not to compare our lives with those of others. We have constant access to the carefully curated aspects of people's lives on Instagram and Pinterest. We get to know about their promotions and awards on LinkedIn. We see their amorphous following on tweeter and the thousands of likes on their posts on Facebook. Instantly, we begin to suffer from a LACK-OF and our lives become WORTH-LESS. We immediately feel less accomplished. Our achievements become meaningless and insignificant in comparison to the big achievements of others. We become sad. And dispirited. Discontent. And insatiable. Sometimes, even depressed.

Remember, dear daughter, that you may seek to learn from and be inspired by the experiences of others. But compete only with yourself. Define for yourself what success means to you. Determine the things that bring you happiness. Do not dwell on comparison or competition, as this will often only make you discontent and disgruntled. If you keep chasing after others, you will one day realise that you have been chasing the wrong things.

*Twenty*
# CHOCOLATE

I KNOW THAT I talked about taking good care of your body. This does not include giving up fine chocolate.

## Twenty-One
# WHAT IS WOMEN FOR WOMEN?

DEAR DAUGHTER, REMEMBER THAT "women for women" does not mean "women against men". You can fiercely love on women without hating men. I am sure that I don't need to explain to you that not all men are evil and that there are many male feminists out there.

## Twenty-Two
# LEARN TO LAUGH AT YOUR MISTAKES

DEAR DAUGHTER, I SPOKE about forgiving yourself for your mistakes. I hope that you also learn to laugh at yourself for some of your mistakes. There are going to be times when you make a fool of yourself. Don't be too hard on yourself. Learn to laugh off this "foolishness" and learn from it. Again, "when you know better, you do better."

## Twenty-Three
# FEEL PAIN BUT DON'T WALLOW IN IT

PAIN AND SADNESS ARE uncomfortable emotions. Naturally, we want to get rid of them. We want to suppress them. Not to feel them. Many times, we numb our pain by ignoring it and shifting our attention to other things, by offloading it onto someone else (usually, a loved one), by drinking to drain our sorrows or medicating to eradicate the misery. We have been taught that we are supposed to be happy. That when we are not happy, there is something wrong with us. Something that we should be afraid of. Something that we need to fix.

Give yourself time to try and understand the genesis of your pain. Be curious about what you are feeling and why you are feeling it. Sit in silence with your pain in spite of the discomfort that it creates. Give yourself permission to cry. Do not dismiss your pain. Do not numb it. Do not ignore it. Do not try to run away from it. Do not rush it. And certainly, do not be ashamed of it. However, try to draw a line between acknowledging and feeling your pain on the one hand and wallowing in it on the other hand. Do not be reduced by your pain. Do not attach yourself to it or let it take over you. Learn from it without feeling a need to be defined by it.

## Twenty-Four
# VALUE YOUR FEMALE FRIENDSHIPS

VALUE AND NURTURE YOUR female friendships. The girlfriends that you pick today will be your sisters tomorrow. The women in your life will celebrate your victories with you and hold space for you when you are experiencing turmoil. They will come and take a ride with you when you buy your first car and cheer you on when you get a promotion at work. They will drive several miles to come and be by your side when you lose a parent and cook meals for you when you have a loved one in hospital. They will mother your children and protect your dignity. They will understand the challenges that you go through as a woman even without you having to explain to them. They will say "I know" and you will know that they know. They will laugh with you and they will cry with you. They will call you to talk about nothing and about everything. And they will show up at your doorstep when you need them, even without you asking.

*Twenty-Five*
# LIFE IS UNCERTAIN

LIFE IS FILLED WITH uncertainties. It is also characterised with pain and punctuated with disappointments. We cannot determine when adversity will visit us. Or indeed can we vaccinate ourselves against it. When adversity does visit you, as it surely will at some point in your life, dial in to God or that which is bigger than yourself. Reach deep into yourself for bearing, lean on the shoulders of loved and trusted friends and family, and if need be, seek professional help.

## Twenty-Six
# PUT THE BAGS DOWN

DEAR DAUGHTER, DO NOT carry around the baggage of bitterness and the stench of hatred. These emotions will only serve to wear you down and tear you apart. Learn whatever lessons you need to learn from those who have betrayed you or caused you pain. And then let go of the toxic emotions that are associated with that trauma.

*Twenty-Seven*
# LIFE IS BEAUTIFUL

THE WORLD IS A beautiful place. There are plenty of wonderful people. There are whole villages and small towns and neighbourhoods and streets filled with people hungry to serve, eager to share and thirsty to connect. Do not let the negative actions of some people contaminate your view of the world and its inhabitants. Do not give in to hopelessness. Continue to entertain the possibility that there is good out there. That tomorrow can and will be better. That love exists. That we are here to thrive.

*Twenty-Eight*
# LOVE AND SERVE
# HUMANITY

TAKE INTEREST IN PEOPLE and not the things that they possess. Treasure family. Make time for friends. Visit the sick and the elderly. Reach out to those in need and comfort those in pain. Exercise your raw humanity without expecting reward or looking for recognition. When you give of yourself and your material possessions, the universe will always find a way of giving back to you.

*Twenty-Nine*

# THE MESSAGE IN
# THE MESSAGE

IT IS IMPORTANT, WHEN receiving feedback, to concentrate on the message in the message. Not everyone is well versed in effective communication. Some people do not even care about the impact of their words. But often, however distasteful the manner in which the feedback is delivered, however vindictive, however uncouth, however unprofessional, there is a message in the message. It is not always necessary to honour the giver of the feedback with a decent response – or any response for that matter. But it is important to reflect on the message and ask yourself: "Is there something in here that I should pay attention to?" "What can I learn from this?" Because, sometimes, there is a lesson in there for you and it will serve you well to pick the lesson out of its poor packaging.

## Thirty
# IT'S OKAY NOT TO KNOW

BE OKAY WITH SAYING "I don't know" or "I do not have an answer to that question." It does not make you any less intelligent to admit that you do not know something. If anything, it opens up opportunities for learning and growth. Be open to new knowledge and curious about people and ideas. Receive constructive criticism with grace and gratitude.

*Thirty-One*

# COMPLIMENT AND CELEBRATE FELLOW WOMEN

COMPLEMENT A FELLOW WOMAN for her gorgeous smile, her brilliant mind, her beautiful dress and her fabulous hair. Celebrate another woman's victories, protect her image from disgrace and uplift her from the trenches of sorrow.

## Thirty-Two
# LEARN TO LET GO

L EARN TO LET GO of things that do not serve you. Relationships that hurt you. Beliefs that belittle you. Thoughts that burden you. Things that crowd your space and your vision. Travel through life with lightness and the buoyancy of a free spirit.

## *Thirty-Three*
## LET GO OF FEAR

DO NOT LET FEAR stop you from acting. Do not let fear keep you from loving. Do not let fear keep you from walking out of an abusive relationship. Do not let fear corner you into hatred. And do not let fear silence you or shut you down.

## Thirty-Four
# DO NOT BE MODEST ABOUT YOUR ACHIEVEMENTS

A S A WOMAN, AND particularly as an African Muslim woman, I was socialised to equate modesty with virtuousness. I was told not to be loud – because ladies do not shout. I was reminded not to talk about my accomplishments because that would seem like boasting – and God does not like proud people. And I was taught not to put my hand up for positions – because that was being too upfront; too pushy. As a result, I learned to downplay my achievements, I lowered – and many times silenced – my voice, and I waited for my turn to be chosen. One day, my supervisor in graduate school told me, "You are very modest Jalia. That's a good thing. Unfortunately, in this market, that does not always work in your favour. When you downplay your achievements, others who have done much less than you, access more opportunities because they are not afraid to talk about their achievements."

Modesty, as Maya Angelou said, is quite different from humility. Maya said, "A modest person will drop the modesty in a minute. You see, it is a learned affectation. But humility comes from the inside out. Humility says, there is someone before me, someone found the path, someone made the road before me, and I have the responsibility of making the road for someone who is yet to come."

So, dear daughter, remember that humility is a much more desirable and admirable virtue. Be humble – not modest. If you have done the work, claim it. You are not showing off. You are simply stating what you have done.

## Thirty-Five
# FORGET PERFECTION

DO THE BEST THAT you can, but do not torture yourself with perfection. The best that you can, will look different on different days, and in different phases of your life. Sometimes, the best that you can, will be meeting all your deadlines and still managing to squeeze in time for exercise and hanging out with friends. Other times, it will be making a big dinner for friends or baking cakes and cookies to share with your neighbours. But there will also be times when the best that you can, will just be making it through the day. And there will be days when the best that you can, will simply be getting out of bed.

Be kind and gentle with yourself. Strive and have high expectations of yourself, knowing that there will be days when you will struggle, even with basics. Focus on getting better and doing better, remembering also that there is a difference between excellence and perfection. Forget perfection. Concentrate instead on giving your best.

## *Thirty-Six*
# MAKE EXCUSES
# FOR PEOPLE

IT IS QUITE EASY for us to judge people who act or look different from us. To sit on a high horse and think "I would never do that". To imagine that we are better than others because we manage our emotions better, we perceive things differently, we have better grades or better jobs and, perhaps, have even achieved what society deems to be appropriate levels of success. But life has taught me again and again that we simply cannot always know what people have been through or what they are going through.

So many people walk around with wounds that are not always visible to us. We do not know whether they have lost a child or a parent, a home or a job. We do not know whether they have been the victims of domestic violence or experienced the rudeness of war. We do not know whether they have just found out that they have cancer or if they are struggling with their mental health. Or simply, that they are just having a bad day. There are many things that we do not know, even about the people that we think we know.

So, as much as possible, make excuses for people. Extend compassion. Be patient. Be kind. However, in doing so, remember also Love Notes 2 (teaching people how to treat you) and 18 (guarding your mental space). Even as you make excuses for others, remember to take care of yourself and to establish healthy boundaries for your own wellbeing.

*Thirty-Seven*

# GIVE UP THE NEED
# TO CONTROL

THERE ARE MANY WAYS in which we try to control people or situations without being aware of our obsession with being in charge. If you had told me some years ago that I was a controlling wife or a controlling mother, I would have looked at you innocently and answered back defensively that I was anything but controlling. But what would explain why I wanted to know exactly what time my husband would be coming back home and what he would be doing the next day? Why would I need him to respond to my text messages the minute he read them, even when they were not urgent? Similarly, as a mother, I have tried to control my children by attempting to nudge them (sometimes not so subtly) in particular directions. The subjects that they should like. The books that they should enjoy reading. The sports that they should favour. Sometimes, even the friends that they should choose.

I rationalised my actions by convincing myself that these were not forms of control. That instead, they came from a place of care, love and concern. This, of course, is partly true. Because I love my husband, I sometimes get concerned when he is not at home in the dark of the night. I think: what if something bad has happened to him? Because I love my children, I care to guide them with my knowledge and to enable them to tap into their full potential.

But it is also true that my actions came from a place of insecurity, a place of fear, a place of wanting to be certain and a place of wanting to know that everything was alright or everything was going be alright. In other words, they came from a place of wanting to control outcomes.

We are normally under the illusion that we can control people or situations. In truth, we have very little control over most things in life. Even the seemingly basic things.

Take the example of my younger daughter. When she was five years old, she was fascinated by the way her older sister joined her letters when she was writing (something that her sister had been taught at school). And so, she tried desperately to copy her sister's handwriting. This resulted in her writing being illegible. I kept trying to get her to get back to her own writing, which for her age, I thought was marvellous. Every time she would try to imitate her sister's handwriting, I would get a piece from her original writing and hold the two against each other and comment on how lovely her original writing was. I would say: "Look at those lovely letters! So easy to read and so beautifully written!" And then I would get the new writing and squint my eyes and say: "Uuuummm, what word is this? It is not as clear as this other really beautiful clear one!"

What did my daughter decide to do? When she was at home, she wrote the way I wanted her to write. But as soon as she got to school, she wrote exactly how she wanted to write. In the evenings, as I looked through her book bag to check whether the school had sent home any communication to parents, I would find small chits of paper where she had written how she wanted to write. Like her sister.

Dear daughter, there are going to be many things in life that you will have little or no control over. The challenges that life throws at you. How people behave towards you. What they think of you. Or indeed what people decide to do with their lives. You will not be able to control the outcomes of many of your actions. You will have little or no control over how a grownup man, or even a child, behaves. And you will not always be able to make people do certain things or think a certain way. Neither will you be able to control whether or not people like you or if they approve of you. The only real control you have is over yourself. Over how you react to how people treat you. Over the things and thoughts that you allow yourself to be consumed by.

So, relax. And breathe.

## Thirty-Eight
## "LEAD YOUR LIFE"

THE LEADERSHIP EXPERT, John Maxwell, once said: "Most people don't lead their lives. They accept their life. And when you accept your life, you are living on things that are not worthy of your time."

For the past six months, I have started my mornings with a practice where I ask myself: How would I like to be remembered? What are the things that bring me joy? What can I do today to move me closer to my goals?

It is easy to blame people and circumstances for all the things that may be going wrong in our lives. But until we can lead our lives, until we can take back control of our lives, until we can stop pointing fingers outside and start searching for answers from inside, we shall spend the bulk of our lives complaining and waiting for people to save us. As much as possible, dear daughter, learn to lead your life. Learn to live a life of purpose. Be a creator of solutions for yourself and for others. Instead of placing blame, ask yourself: how can I bring change to this situation? What is in my power? Sometimes, we can only do very little to change situations. But many times, that little goes a long way.

## Thirty-Nine
# HAVE A SOURCE
# OF INCOME

WHEN I WAS IN graduate school, I lived with a young couple – Annette and Esau – who I now fondly call my sister and brother. At the time, they had a two-year old son. Because Annette wanted to work, but also spend time with their son, she got a job at a child-care centre in a gym, where she could take her son along. I once asked Annette why she felt the need to work when Esau was earning enough money to comfortably take care of them and was quite happy to provide financially for his family. It was not as if the pay at the gym was great, anyway. Annette responded that it was not really about the money. It was about the dignity and sense of independence that came from earning an income.

Even though she was not earning much, whenever she got paid, Annette would pass by the *Young Brothers* store, which sold fresh fruits and vegetables. She would come home with shopping bags filled with kale and broccoli, and avocado and grapes, and strawberries and watermelons. Every now and then, she would treat us all to an afternoon out at the local *Starbucks* where we got our pick of hot chocolate or caramel macchiato, accompanied with slices of banana bread and blueberry muffins. Today, over ten years later, even after earning her Masters degree, Annette still chooses to spend the bulk of her time with their three energetic handsome sons. However, she also still finds gigs that would allow her to earn an income.

Dear daughter, if it is possible, it is important that you earn an income of your own, however little it is. An income that will allow you the simple luxury of treating yourself to little pleasures and the dignity to afford basic necessities. An income that will allow you to treat yourself to a cup of hot chocolate at a coffee shop on a cold winter afternoon. An income that will enable you to afford to buy basic necessities such as sanitary pads and bras and underpants. An income that will give you permission to gift yourself with a good book and save up for a trip to a place that you have longed to travel to. An income that will enable you to pay your bills and invest in your dreams. An income that will assist you to walk out of an abusive relationship and provide you with shelter on rainy days.

*Forty*

# AFTER DARKNESS,
# COMES LIGHT

ALMOST EVERY MORNING, from Monday to Friday, at about 6am, I step out of the house for a long walk. It is not always pleasant leaving the house at that time of day, particularly in the colder months. I am engulfed in a cloak of darkness. The biting cold pierces my half-asleep body. A dead silence occupies the streets. And on days like today, there is a heavy downpour of rain threatening to dampen my spirit.

Still, I walk out. I have been here before. And I know that if I continue walking, in spite of how I am feeling, I will meet with light. At the bottom of Roedale Road, I will peep into the No. 50 bus and wonder whether the passengers are heading back home or heading to work. At Preston Road, I will watch with appreciation the gentleman who is dutifully in service, sweeping away the fallen leaves and scattered litter, his bright yellow hi-vis jacket flashing against the dark. I will admire the commitment of the elderly gentleman who is always already deeply buried in his work by the time I walk past his bright-lit shop at 6.30am.

I am no longer aware of the darkness. I smile through the droplets of rain sitting on my eyelids. I look forward to meeting the beautiful lady with the purple tint in her hair, whose generous smile and jolly "good morning!" never fail to cheer me up. I notice that the darkness has lifted and in its place is the sight of a colony of seagulls, squabbling in the centre of Preston Park, their white feathers gathered in a beautiful contrast to the thick greenery. I listen keenly to the chirping of birds in the trees, watch as dogs animatedly run around the fields and notice fellow humans who have arisen for yet another day. As I walk past the local bakery, I am met with the sweet smell of freshly baking bread and the aroma of roasted almond croissants.

A different kind of silence embraces me. A silence of peace. A silence of hope. The promise that is wrapped in each new day.

Dear daughter, as you journey through life, you are bound to experience seasons of darkness. Periods in your life when things are not going the way you would want them to go. Moments when you will experience great loss and carry around the burden of a heavy heart. There may be times when you will wonder, "Is this all there is to life?" "Is this even worth it?"

This, dear daughter, is life. It has happy moments and sad moments. It has sunny days and cloudy days. There are seasons of merry making and there are seasons of grief. There are days when everything seems to go well and there are days when nothing seems to go well. There are days that are memorable and there are days that are painfully dull. I would like to think, however, that on the whole, we get to experience more light than we do darkness. And often times, our perspective of things determines whether we see the light or whether we are stuck in the dark.

This year – 2020 – has been a particularly tough year for the majority of people around the world. The coronavirus pandemic has dealt us a heavy blow. We have buried our loved ones along with our dreams. We have lost jobs and cancelled long-planned celebrations. We have experienced wider income disparities and witnessed greater divisions along lines of race. We are wandering through a thicket of uncertainty, unable to visualise an end date. We do not know when we will be able to enjoy simple pleasures such as hanging out with a group of friends without worrying about catching a virus. We do not know when we will be able to visit our loved ones. To sit around dining tables to enjoy big family meals and inside jokes. Millions have lost jobs and businesses have closed shop, without guarantees about when or indeed, whether, their sources of livelihood will be restored. In countries like Uganda, my home country, public schools have been closed for almost a year. We do not know when all children will be able to go back to school. For some children, particularly girls, this period has marked the end of their education journey. School will be no more. Even in developed countries, such as England, the loss of jobs has meant that more families are turning to food banks for a basic meal for their children.

A blanket of darkness hovers over us.

And yet, as a human collective, we have been here before. Many times. Whether it has been wars or famine or health pandemics, we have pushed through tremendous hardships and somehow come out on the other side. The resilience of the human spirit has enabled us to imagine and rebuild better futures, in spite of our brokenness.

For the first time, I am able to truly comprehend the story that I was told many years ago about my maternal grandfather. Sometime in the 1920s, when Abi (as he was fondly called by friends and family) was still a young man, a plague attacked the village in which he and his family lived. His mother, his wife and his cousin all caught the plague and died instantly. Abi was not around at the time of their deaths, all of which happened within a very short period of each other. When he returned to the village, he found three dead bodies. He was devastated. His agony was intensified when he failed to convince his relatives to help him with the burial arrangements. They feared that if they were to engage in burial, they too would catch the plague and die.

Abi had a friend called Abdallah Kubebba, who was a Muslim. He went to Abdallah's house crying and narrated his ordeal. As he walked away, his face buried in tears, Abdallah pulled him back and hugged him, telling him to stay strong. After Abi left, Abdallah reached out to members of the Muslim community, telling them that a young man had suffered great loss and that it would be good if

they could come together to support him. The
Muslims convened. They washed the bodies of the
dead, prayed for them and buried them. Abi was so
moved and humbled by the actions of these people,
many of whom he barely knew. Henceforth, a
strong bond was birthed between him and the
Muslims; one that resulted in his conversion to
Islam. By the time of his death, Abi was one of the
most prominent Muslims in Uganda. He was
revered, not just for his contributions to Islam and
the Muslim community, but more broadly, for his
contributions to Ugandans and to humanity: the
schools that he constructed, the children and adults
that he sponsored to obtain an education, the
teachers and school administrators whose salaries he
paid, the financial assistance that he provided to
those who were experiencing economic hardship
and, even, the men for whom he paid graduated
tax, a local tax imposed on all men above the age of
18.

During a very dark period in his life, people
that Abi barely knew showed up for him in the

most humane way and lit a torch in him. This torch would in turn provide lighting for thousands and hundreds of thousands of people in the decades to come.

While I had heard this story several times before, reflecting on it in the midst of the coronavirus pandemic has given it new meaning. I had never fully understood how Abi's relatives could fail to help with the burial of their own relatives. I did not appreciate the level of anxiety and the sense of helplessness that can grip a community and render it paralysed. I never imagined that there would be a time in my lifetime when we could fail to hug a loved one when they were hurting. I would never have foreseen a situation where our interactions would be restricted, in a free world. Where wearing masks in public would become normalised. Where we talked to our loved ones while standing six feet apart. Where our children would not be able to go into school for several months, not because they were sick, but because the environment was sick.

And yet, here we are. Unable to plan for tomorrow because we are just trying to make it through today.

But just like it happened during Abi's time, as a result of this pandemic, I have also seen how communities have come together to take care of each other. For many of us, the pandemic has reminded us that we were made for connection. I have seen how people have collected care packages for those who are confined to their homes. I have seen how younger people have taken care of the elderly in their communities. I have seen how people have refused to see their fellow humans go hungry. I have heard of people who have cooked food for the sick, collected donations for the homeless and baked cakes to raise money for meals for those who are struggling financially. And I have witnessed how people have chosen kindness and hope in spite of the hopelessness that surrounds them.

Abi's story reassures me that this too shall pass. We shall find solutions to the virus. The sun will shine again. We shall be able to commune again. And maybe our connections will be even more meaningful.

If Abi's story seems like it was centuries ago, then I have felt compelled to nibble on the story of my own mother. As a young woman, in the 1980s, she fled Uganda with her husband and her young children to escape the war. She left behind her beloved father, Abi, her heartbroken mother, her siblings, her friends and her home. She was plucked away from the sense of security that comes from the place that one is birthed and bred. The familiarity of language, the soils that grew her staple food, her thriving businesses. In neighbouring Kenya, she would not only have to make new friends and learn new languages, but she would also have to live with the losses that she would never physically witnesses. Her father, who was her best friend, died. She did not get to bury him. Her mother died. She did not get to bury her. Her siblings and friends died. She did not get to bury them. Again and again, her delicate heart was pierced and punched. On several occasions, she had mental breakdowns.

Many years later, she told us that the only thing that kept her going was her children. When she knelt on her mat to say her prayers, she asked God to just keep her alive long enough so she could see her children grow and finish school. Today, she does not only enjoy the gift of her healthy and thriving children, but she is also immersed in the joy of grandchildren. She lives around the same neighbourhood where she grew up, close to her siblings. Shortly after returning to Uganda, she opened a business, which was a great success. She was able to laugh again and hope again.

I do not tell you these stories to diminish what you may be feeling right now. Fear. Anxiety. Disappointment. Sadness. Heartbreak. Maybe even anger. Your feelings are valid. We have, individually and collectively, experienced great loss. We are grieving.

I tell you these stories to remind both you and I of the resilience of the human spirit. That even as the alleys of 2020 have been starkly dark, there are still glimmers of hope. We are the hope – you and I. And we cannot afford to give in to hopelessness. We need to hold space for each other. We need to look at each other and look out for each other. We need to lean on each other and extend our hearts to each other. We shall overcome. And if we do this right, we shall be the better for it.

When a blanket of darkness spreads over you, when unhappiness seeps into the pores of your being, when you experience the unfortunate encounter with grave hardship, seek comfort in the knowledge that after darkness comes light and following hardship is ease. In the meantime, be awake to the universe of beings that are consciously or subconsciously conspiring for your good. It will be well.

# LOVE, FROM A FATHER

1. Yes, I am a grown man. Older and wiser as the adage goes. But I don't know everything, may forget some things and won't always understand you as accurately as you feel. There are some things you may know that I won't and things you feel that I may never experience (like your periods). There are encounters you may find yourself in that I haven't exactly had to deal with. Just know that you can talk to me about life. That I will always be there to support and protect you as best as I can. Let's communicate about what we would like from each other. It doesn't mean you will always get what you want. If I do not seem to understand, please feel free to tell me what to do. I will take it as guidance rather than an order. Talk to

me... or let me just give you a hug when in turmoil; no need to talk sometimes. We may not be on the exact same page, but we are in the same book (of life), just different editions. I love you.

2. Be aware that you embody mother nature in her perfectly imperfect way. The parts of your body you may be anxious about are the same parts that appeal to many people. The hesitation that grows inside you when weighing whether to do some things is nature's way of protecting you and others. Never mind if you can't succinctly articulate how you feel or why you feel that way. We, men, often confuse logic for rationality and can get impatient when the response we desire is not forthcoming. Many modern societies also frequently confuse intelligence and wisdom, inclining people to quick decision making as opposed to taking time to process information and making the right decisions. Life is neither a business nor a

race. Do good by others but be good to yourself first. Do not feel selfish about doing good by you.

3. There is a difference between joy and happiness. Many things and people may make you happy but genuine joy, only you can originate. Because you are reading this book, you have life, you can read or hear, you have the capacity to process the content, and so much more. Whenever you feel despondent, feel around you and smile at the little flowers growing between stones, the insects buzzing about, birds chirping, the food aromas, the different colours around you, people laughing, textures and songs of life. Marvel at your own growth. Painful experiences are necessary and will certainly happen. Suffering from them is an option which is unnecessary. An example of pain is your periods. An example of suffering is resenting it and wondering why it has to be so painful for you.

4. Power: You should have power over yourself if you want to flourish using it to influence others. You may occasionally feel certain ways (good or bad) because of what other people say. In those moments, you will have ceded power over to them. Your power lies in your gentleness. Nature made you appear relatively fragile to most men and patriarchy has mischaracterised you as the 'weaker sex'. Do not fall into the trap of trying to express power using male yardsticks. Your strength lies in your vulnerability. You can make your voice heard without shouting. You can make your sentiments felt without being unkind. Even your silence speaks volumes.

5. Love is not blind like the fictional music, books and movies suggest. To love blindly is a failure to exercise your ability to judge character or indeed be conscious of who and what is good for you. I still do not understand why people 'fall in love' for falling is usually accidental and certainly never a good thing. Falling connotes

losing control and often those who fall hurt themselves. When getting into something, it is important that you be aware that you have control over how to feel and what to do when and where. A woman with little or no self-control is most attractive to controlling people. Showing self-control will earn you trust from those who genuinely care about you.

6.  Cleanliness is spiritual. It can range from personal hygiene to your surroundings. It will protect your health as well as garner respect from others. Good hygiene will also earn you trust as it reflects the character of someone that takes personal responsibility.

7.  Love and respect your mother. She may not necessarily always represent to you what you would like to see but she is your root. You will have difficulty growing well and flourishing as a tree if you feel sour towards her. No tree bears good fruit if not firmly rooted; it may distort the energy you pass onto the next

generation. If there has been friction, try to make peace. I feel like emphasising this again. Please love your mother. She loves you more than anyone else you can think of or will ever meet.

8. There is a difference between being a unique individual and a special person. We are all unique individuals but when we start feeling special, we gravitate towards expecting others to treat us as such. You are entitled to respect but not to special treatment.

9. Do not skimp on good food. You may compromise about other expenditures but never on healthy food.

10. Money is good, but it can be corrupting. Be careful from who you accept it and how you earn it. It is a sort of transfer of energy. If one earns it through harming others, sharing it with you means they will transfer part of their burden of making amends to you. Work hard and smart so you do not have to depend on

others, although there is nothing wrong with interdependence with good people.

11. Men are nice. Some can get extra nice when they want something, like sex. It doesn't necessarily make them bad for wanting it, but they don't really fully understand what it means or feels like for you. Giving it to them will make them happy (momentarily) but it doesn't mean they will necessarily respect nor like you more. Some may even feel entitled or regard you as a conquest if you engage in such with them. They respect you even if you don't engage in it (usually more as you have demonstrated self-respect, drawn clear boundaries and demonstrated that you are aware that women hold the power in such encounters). Having sex (especially unprotected) has a lot of consequences for you that you should try to understand. Emotional, psychological and even physiological. When you are ready, you will be able to engage in it in a more empowering way.

12. I am probably the only man that will do just about anything for you and want absolutely nothing in return, so utilise me. I say probably because even I would hope you do little things like check on me in my old age.

13. Love yourself. You can be self-centred without being selfish. A healthy and flourishing you is good for you and those that interact with you. If something negatively affects your well-being, refrain from it. Engaging in it to fit in or please others is going to unsettle you afterwards. Those that incline you towards it may accept you into their sphere, but they are not going to respect you more for breaching your own values. Try to define a simple set of values for yourself and maintain those boundaries.

14. Be curious. Do not stop being inquisitive about society, your heritage and your environment. Always think WHY things are as they seem, WHY you are being advised to

behave a certain way, WHY people say no, WHY people suggest something is good or bad for you.

15. The future: don't worry about it. Be excited about it. If you do get worried, share your worries with me in their raw form and let's explore different perspectives of them together. I can share mine too, if you are interested.

16. I love you and always will. Home is always open.

# LASTLY, "DO NOT DIE WITH YOUR MUSIC STILL INSIDE YOU"

DEAR DAUGHTER, WHEN I walked into my first class in law school over 20 years ago, I had the precious gifts of youthful zeal and unencumbered idealism. As far as I was concerned, I was going to use the law to change the world. I would ensure that single mothers, like my own, were not dispossessed of their property by greedy male relatives. I would employ the law to protect small business owners from harsh government regulations and wave it like a magic wand to eliminate suppression and oppression. The law, as I understood it, was about honouring truth, protecting the vulnerable and righting wrongs. To be honest, I also rather liked the idea of wearing a crisply ironed suit and sitting in a high-rise air-conditioned office.

However, I soon realised that my idea of how the law works was perhaps too romanticised, having relied (perhaps too heavily) on the American legal dramas that I watched on television. I would later discover that, in practice, legal institutions failed to uphold justice and that even when justice was served, it was often times delayed. I found that I had neither the tenacity nor the strength of heart to watch the slow wheels of justice and even worse, injustice clothed as justice. I decided to pursue a Master of Laws and, later, a PhD in Law, believing that if I piled on more degrees, I would not only acquire more knowledge (which would enable me to better contribute to the changes that I wanted to see in society), but also that I would feel more valued and more valuable. Of all areas of the law, I chose taxation.

In a few cases, I did actually tell the kinds of stories that I had always wanted to tell. Stories about how to reduce taxes on goods produced with inputs sourced from local farmers. Stories about how to build more equitable tax systems by ensuring that wealthy people paid their fair share in taxes. Stories about how tax systems could be used to improve the livelihoods of women. And stories that unpacked the manner in which laws further marginalised already vulnerable people. In a small way, I felt that the stories that I was telling, even though often clothed in unfashionable tax jargon, were making some contribution to a just and equitable society.

For the most part, however, I was haunted by my unfed desires, which frequently visited me, even as I tried to push them to the back burner. I had convinced myself that I needed to live in the "real world" – a world that made my desires seem like childish fantasies. I had convinced myself that I had to choose a singular path: in this case, be a serious academic. I craved for the child in me; the dreamer in me. The child who loved to sing at the top of her lungs and run around, barefooted, chasing after her younger siblings. The child who climbed trees and composed songs. The child who was guided by her heart and not necessarily by her mind. The teenager who, together with her high school best friend, Rachel, wrote novels stuffed with fantasies. The teenager who, along with her soul sister, Nuruh, would sit on top of their double-decker beds at Nabisunsa Girls School and make plans for COTW – Children of the World – an organisation that we would establish to ensure that destitute children were moved off the streets of Kampala into classrooms, to increase the chances of their futures bearing some semblance to our futures.

I missed the dreamer. The believer. The one who allowed herself to feel and hope. The one who was not burdened by proved theories and statistical certainties. Somewhere along the way, this child had died. This child grew up and internalised the message that her dreams were not valid and that her songs needed to be buried. This child was made to believe that to grow up meant to stop dreaming, to give up singing, to numb feelings and to exile passion. Finish university. Get a job. Get married. Have children. Maybe buy a house. Exist.

To conform to the rules of engagement in adulthood, I adapted an identity that in many ways conflicted with my inner child. I had to be seen as the intelligent – and serious – woman, who was an academic. I equated my intelligence (and my worth) with my ability to publish articles in reputable journals, to speak at international conferences and to be cited as an authority in my field of work. I worked hard at receiving public affirmations and recognitions. How many times had an article that I had written been cited or downloaded? What happened when I searched for my name in Google? What kinds of conferences was I invited to speak at? On the professional network, LinkedIn, I obsessively refreshed my page to see how many people had sent me invitations to connect, how many people had viewed my profile in the past 12 hours and how many people had liked something that I had posted.

News of other people's achievements would send me into a silent panic and dampen my days because I felt like I was being left behind. In this panic, I started chasing after things that I was not really interested in because I wanted to be recognised, to be seen, to belong. Needless to say, many of these things did not nourish me. And to be sure, they did not belong to me. Even worse, chasing after them meant that I numbed and suppressed my deepest and truest yearnings.

The spiritual teacher, Wayne Dyer, said "Do not die with your music inside you." For several years, I have muted my music in pursuit of what others deem to be the emblems of success. I have climbed professional ladders and waited on gatekeepers of "success" to give me permission to be. I have been afraid to share with the world the parts of myself that nourish my spirit, believing that

I needed to choose to be just one thing. That I could not occupy multiple identities.

This little book of love is in some ways a rebellion against conformity. Finally, I have gathered the courage to sing out of my own hymn book. To undress myself of technical jargon without worrying about whether I sound academic enough or intelligent enough. To speak directly to my audience, without the filter of a broker. To seek not the permission of a publisher to gain entry into the literary world. To draw on the youthful enthusiasm and infectious passion of three talented and hardworking young ladies – Martha Omasoro, Alliance Nsenga and Pascale Nsenga (the designers of the book cover) – as a reminder to myself of the validity of our dreams and the importance of keeping them alive.

Naturally, because I am a product of habit and because I have habitually questioned the intelligence of my ideas and the value of my contributions, there is that internal critic who mocks me: *Who do you think you are? What new thing do you have to say that has not been said before? Also, seriously, who chooses a title as corny as "Love Notes to a Dear Daughter"? Like… really?* There's another voice. A kinder voice. A voice that is as unsure as it is idealistic. It says: *Why shouldn't you share your ideas? Who said you need permission to sing your songs? Who are you to determine whether your ideas will speak to someone and how they will speak to them? Also, if you are going to tell your two little daughters that their dreams are valid, you better live by example.* I choose this second voice. I choose to believe that my ideas are worthy. I choose to share them without any guarantees of how they will be received, but, knowing that *this is my music.* I get to sing it. I hope that you too give yourself permission to sing your songs, dear daughter.

Printed in Great Britain
by Amazon